CREATING

# HAWAIIAN-INSPIRED QUILTS

## JUDITH SANDSTROM

4880 Lower Valley Road · Atglen, PA 19310

# DEDICATION

I dedicate this book to my husband Frank

—who kindly and expertly photographed all my quilts—

for his patience, companionship, and enduring love.

# ACKNOWLEDGMENTS

I would like to acknowledge the invaluable assistance of Carol Kamaile

in assembling the magnificent collection of modern Hawaiian quilts.

Carol's *Hibiscus Fire* featured on the back cover shows the type of

Hawaiian quilt that inspired my designs.

Type set in Garamond /Cinzel Decorative

ISBN: 978-0-7643-4858-7

Printed in China

Published by Schiffer Publishing, Ltd.

4880 Lower Valley Road | Atglen, PA 19310
Phone: (610) 593-1777; Fax: (610) 593-2002
E-mail: Info@schifferbooks.com

For our complete selection of fine books on this and related subjects, please visit our website at www. schifferbooks.com. You may also write for a free catalog.

This book may be purchased from the publisher. Please try your bookstore first.

We are always looking for people to write books on new and related subjects. If you have an idea for a book, please contact us at proposals@schifferbooks.com.

Schiffer Publishing's titles are available at special discounts for bulk purchases for sales promotions or premiums. Special editions, including personalized covers, corporate imprints, and excerpts can be created in large quantities for special needs. For more information, contact the publisher.

# CONTENTS

Introduction   4

History of Hawaiian Quilts   5

Work of Modern Quilt Makers   6

Basic Supplies, General Directions,
Binding Directions   16

CHAPTER 1:
**Traditional Single-Color Designs**   17

*Hawaiian Seas*   18

*Scallop Shell and Starfish, Angel Fish and Coral,
Crab and Stingray, Turtle and Jellyfish*   19

*Hawaiian Christmas* with Four Blocks   20

CHAPTER 2:
**Traditional Center-Embellished
with Added Colors**   23

*Christmas Cactus*   24

*Hibiscus and Tulip Bouquet*   27

*May Maze*   30

CHAPTER 3:
**Embellished Block-Used
Repeated Times**   32

*Butterfly Trails*   33

*Four Color Tulips*   36

*Tahitian Dream*   38

CHAPTER 4:
**Embellished Block-Center Medallion
with Patchwork**   41

*Exotic Purple Lily*   42

*Amazing Amaryllis*   46

*Daffodils and Bluebirds*   50

CHAPTER 5:
**Patterns**   54

Directions for Cutting and Stitching
Hand-Appliquéd Hawaiian Blocks   54

Directions for Cutting and Stitching
Machine-Appliquéd Hawaiian Blocks   56

Sewing Patterns   57-80

# INTRODUCTION

The early nineteenth century Hawaiian women were introduced to quilting by the missionaries who came to their lovely islands. Rather than stitching together small pieces of fabric, they chose to fashion their unique designs around the indigenous flowers and plants. By folding a large piece of fabric into quarters or eighths, they could cut flowing motifs symbolic of their lush environment. Because material was scarce, they used the bright, solid colors brought to their islands by merchants. The practice of using one single piece of solid color fabric appliquéd onto a white background became their tradition.

The same techniques used by early Hawaiian quilters are still used today in an effort to preserve and perpetuate their tradition. The following images show the flowing appliquéd designs and magnificent hand quilting that embody true Hawaiian quilts. The following quilts, made by Silvia Bredeson in the traditional manner, are the type that inspire and stimulate my own creativity.

*Pua Pake*
quilt made by Silvia Bredeson, designed by Poakalani.

Although the early Hawaiian designs were inspired primarily by flowers and trees, I have portrayed small sea creatures in my Hawaiian Seas wall quilts. I have used subtle prints and tone-on-tone fabrics with texture, rather than solids in my designs and often tan backgrounds rather than white. Many of my designs have a decidedly American feel, and my flowers are tulips, lilies, amaryllis, and daffodils, with an occasional hibiscus in the mix. Only one design in the book, May Maze, is echo quilted in the traditional Hawaiian style, but each block has been hand-appliquéd out of respect for the time-honored Hawaiian tradition.

If you love the look of Hawaiian hand-appliqué, but have neither the time nor inclination to attempt it, my cutting method lends itself perfectly to machine appliqué. You are able to achieve a very similar appearance without the labor-intensive hand work. I offer directions for both hand and machine appliqué in Chapter 5: Patterns and Directions for Cutting and Stitching.

I have shown a progression from the traditional Hawaiian style to my own interpretations. I incorporate the symmetrical appliquéd center with added motifs and colors combined with patchwork blocks and borders. The designs range in size from a 27"square wall quilt to a 70"x 98" bed quilt. Patterns and directions are provided for all of the projects. I hope you will find something appealing to stitch and will be inspired, as I am, by the Hawaiian style quilt.

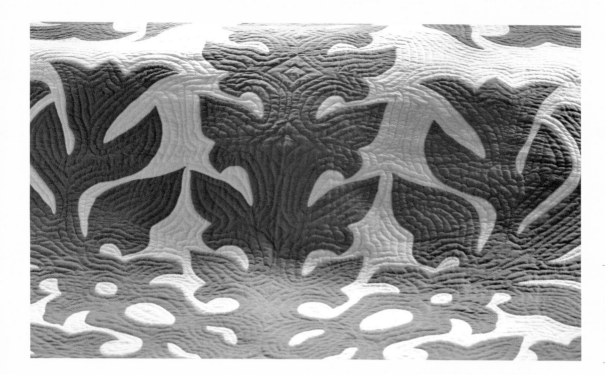

*Winds of Waimea* quilt made by Silvia Bredeson, designed by Sonja "Konia" Oberosler.

# HISTORY OF HAWAIIAN QUILTS

Early Hawaiian people made cloth called kapa from the inner bark of native mulberry trees. They beat and felted the bark until it became soft and supple. Their first bed-covering consisted of layers of kapa sewn with needles made from shells or plant materials. The top layer was decorated with stamped geometric designs.

By the 1820s, missionaries had come to the Hawaiian Islands, bringing metal needles and scraps of cotton fabric. Although the Hawaiians were hesitant to use the fabric scraps in patchwork quilts, they used them to decorate their kapa.

By 1870, solid-color cotton fabric had been imported and was readily available. This marked the advent of the traditional Hawaiian quilt. A large piece of fabric was folded in eighths or quarters and cut in a symmetrical design. It was then hand-appliquéd onto a contrasting solid-color background. A red design appliquéd onto a white background was a popular choice because those colors were in the greatest supply. The traditional method of intricate echo quilting radiating outward from the appliquéd design was the quilting method of choice and still remains so today.

The designs were inspired by nature, such as a flower or plant. Sometimes a special event or spiritual occurrence in the life of the quilt maker became the inspiration. Many believe that the breadfruit pattern was the first design and symbolized a fruitful life. It was thought that each quilt contained the spirit of the maker. In the past, many quilts were burned upon the death of their creator to allow her spirit to pass on with her.

By the 1890s, several quilts incorporated the flag of Hawaii and symbols of Hawaiian royalty. These recorded the history of the monarchy prior to its overthrow in 1893. Crazy quilts and embroidered quilts were also made during this time period.

The Hawaiian quilt is a sacred part of the Hawaiian culture. The traditional quilt makers never shared their creations until they were completed, and many were passed from one generation to the next to be viewed only by their family members. Modern quilt makers attempt to carry on the legacy with their own interpretation of traditional patterns.

# WORK OF MODERN QUILT MAKERS

In order to illustrate the type of traditional Hawaiian quilts that inspired my own creations, my husband Frank and I booked a cruise from Los Angeles to the Hawaiian Islands. Through prior correspondence with Hawaiian quilt guilds, museums, and shops, I was able to locate the wonderful quilters whose work is featured herein.

All of these women generously shared their time, stories, and lovely quilts with us. Carol Kamaile, president of the Hawaii Quilt Guild and a Master Quilter of Hawaiian quilting, organized a group of her students from Oahu. We met in the Honolulu home of one of the quilters and were permitted to photograph their magnificent work. Frank and I were truly honored to be invited into such a vibrant and friendly group.

When we arrived in Hilo on the Big Island, Silvia Bredeson and her husband Allan picked us up in their car. They had already driven two hours in the rain from the opposite side of the island to get us. Once in the car, we were driven another forty minutes to the home of their friends, Jerry and Cindy Andersen, in the lovely rain forest of Pahoa. Although strangers, we were welcomed as friends and given a tour of their magnificent home and grounds. There we photographed Silvia's two incredible bed quilts. Afterward, Allan and Silvia drove us back to the cruise terminal before returning to their home two hours away. This is a fine example of the true "Aloha" spirit.

Each of the quilts pictured here illustrates the traditional Hawaiian method of folding, cutting, and appliqué, as well as the echo quilting—all done entirely by hand. Frank and I feel privileged indeed to have had the honor of meeting these lovely women who perpetuate the time-honored Hawaiian quilting tradition. It is with great sorrow that we mourn the sudden passing of Barbara Kato, one of our quilting friends in Oahu.

Carol Kamaile        Jeannie Salmon        Linda Orion

Dee Valentine        Barbara Kato        Silvia Bredeson

*Hibiscus.*
108" x 108" queen size made
by Linda Orion for her daughter's
wedding, designed by
Carol Kamaile. *Photo courtesy
of Matthew Hirata.*

*Lehua.*

45" x 45" wall quilt made by
Linda Orion, designed by
Carol Kamaile. *Photo courtesy
of Matthew Hirata.*

*Monstera Wild.*
108" x 108" queen size made
and designed by Jeannie Salmon.
Won "Best in Show" at the
2009 Kahala Mall show.
*Photo courtesy of Matthew Hirata.*

*Monstera 2.*
Double-size sister quilt to
*Monstera Wild* made and designed
by Jeannie Salmon. *Photo courtesy
of Matthew Hirata.*

*Kaleo Aloha.*
Full quilt with pillow top design. Made by Jeannie Salmon, designed by Elizabeth Akana. Named after the Naupaka plant that grows by the ocean. *Photo courtesy of Matthew Hirata.*

*Garden of Angels.*
Double bed quilt with floating border inspired by the Angel Trumpet plant. Made and designed by Jeannie Salmon. *Photo courtesy of Matthew Hirata.*

*Hibiscus Fire.*
60"x 60" Hibiscus and Maile Lei design with a very unusual center kaleidoscope using a Hawaiian print. Made and designed by Carol Kamaile, this quilt won first place at the 2010 Hawaii Quilt Guild show. *Photo courtesy of Matthew Hirata.*

*Ho'o Pumehana Hibiscus.*
Made and designed by Carol Kamaile. *Photo courtesy of Matthew Hirata.*

*Pothos.*
Wall quilt reminiscent of a philodrendon made and designed by Carol Kamaile. *Photo courtesy of Matthew Hirata.*

*Rainbow of Gingers.*
58½" x 48" wall quilt with a Micronesian Ginger Lei center and floating red ginger border, batik on yellow. Made and designed by Carol Kamaile, this quilt won second place at the 2011 "Hawaii Quilt Guild" show. *Photo courtesy of Matthew Hirata.*

*Ho'o Pumehana Monstera.*
Made and designed by Carol Kamaile.
*Photo courtesy of Matthew Hirata.*

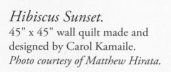

*Hibiscus Sunset.*
45" x 45" wall quilt made and
designed by Carol Kamaile.
*Photo courtesy of Matthew Hirata.*

*E Komo Mai.*
A Monstera door quilt that means: "Welcome, Come In."
Made and designed by Carol Kamaile.
*Photo courtesy of Matthew Hirata.*

*Ho'o Pumehana Anthurium.*

Twin-sized bed quilt with floating Maile Lei border.
Made by Barbara Kato and designed by Carol Kamaile.
*Photo courtesy of Matthew Hirata.*

*Waikaloa Beauty.*
Wall quilt made and designed
by Jeannie Salmon.
*Photo courtesy of Matthew Hirata.*

*Ho'o Pumehana Plumeria.*
Lovely quit with fallen plumeria flowers in the corners.
Made by Barbara Kato and designed by Carol Kamaile.
*Photo courtesy of Matthew Hirata.*

*My Father's Garden.*
Wall quilt with Anthurium motif made and designed by Jeannie Salmon. *Photo courtesy of Matthew Hirata.*

*Niu, Coconut Tree.*
67" x 108" (January 2010–June 2011) made by Emiko Ouye, designed by Carol Kamaile. *Photo courtesy of Matthew Hirata.*

# BASIC SUPPLIES

Rotary cutter, self-healing mat, and acrylic ruler

Needles for hand-appliqué and hand quilting

Thread to match all appliqué fabrics

Hand quilting thread

Fine point pen for tracing patterns

Manila folders or template material for making patterns

Small sharp fabric scissors

Scissors for cutting paper

Lightweight fusible web for machine-appliquéd blocks

Lightweight fusible interfacing for machine-appliquéd blocks

Iron and ironing board

# GENERAL DIRECTIONS

Use fine quality cotton fabric throughout, but especially for the appliqué pieces. The sample quilts utilize mostly tone-on-tone fabrics rather than solids to provide additional depth and texture. Pre-wash and iron all fabrics before cutting.

Use the rotary cutting tools for all straight-edge patchwork pieces, and small sharp scissors for the appliqué pieces. Rotary cut the strips, squares, and triangles first, and then cut the small appliqué pieces from the remaining fabric. All appliqué patterns are found in the Pattern Section and are marked with the color and number required. Follow the directions in the Pattern Section to baste and stitch the appliquéd blocks using the needle turn appliqué method. When one pattern piece is placed on top of another, baste and appliqué the smaller piece onto the larger one before stitching the larger piece onto the block or center panel.

Note that the seam allowance for all patchwork is ¼" and all seams are pressed open. The directions for patchwork construction appear with the individual designs. Thoroughly press the quilt top as it is stitched. Sandwich the batting between the completed top and the backing that has been washed and ironed. Hand baste the three layers together in vertical and horizontal rows. Baste around the perimeter.

Each project in the book has been quilted by hand. The *May Maze* design has been echo quilted in the style of traditional Hawaiian quilts but more densely. The Hawaiian echo quilting rows are an index finger in width apart. Always begin quilting in the center and work outward to the edges. Outline the appliquéd design by quilting very close to the hand stitching around all the motifs. Accentuate the borders and patchwork sections by quilting ¼" from the seam lines so the quilting is evenly spaced and the quilt lies flat. Remove the interior basting after the quilting has been completed, leaving the perimeter. Trim the batting and backing even with the quilt top.

# BINDING DIRECTIONS

Stitch together the 2" binding strips (the number designated by design) into one long strip. Fold the strip in half lengthwise with the wrong side inside. Align the binding with the basted quilt top. With raw edges together, stitch the binding to the quilt top using a ¼" seam allowance. Stop stitching ¼" from the corner, reposition the binding, and begin stitching the next side ¼" from the corner. Stitch the binding ends together and miter the corners. Turn the binding to the back of the quilt and blind stitch it into place.

# CHAPTER I

## TRADITIONAL SINGLE-COLOR DESIGNS

These quilts most closely resemble the appearance
and feeling of traditional Hawaiian quilts, although the subjects
encompass non-traditional sea life and symbols of Christmas.
I have used flowing tone-on-tone fabrics and added dramatic floral
and pieced borders to accentuate the blocks.
The fabrics used in the Hawaiian Seas wall quilts were
actually manufactured and purchased in Hawaii.

# HAWAIIAN SEAS

## A COLLECTION OF FOUR WALL QUILTS: 27" X 27"

*Turtle and Jellyfish | Scallop Shell and Starfish | Crab and Stingray | Angel Fish and Coral*
Wall quilts from the Hawaiian Seas collection.

## MATERIALS

Note that yardages and directions are given for one wall quilt. They are identical for each of the four.

⅝ yd. off-white

½ yd. dark blue

¼ yd. large print

¼ yd. fabric for binding

30" square of thin cotton batting

⅞ yd. backing fabric

## CUTTING DIRECTIONS

From the off-white, cut the following:

(1) 20½" square

From the dark blue, cut the following:

(4) 4" squares

From the large print, cut the following:

(2) 4" x 44" strips—cut each strip in half and trim each half strip to 4" x 20½".

From the binding fabric, cut the following:

(3) 2" x 44" strips

## SEWING DIRECTIONS

Refer to the Pattern Section for directions to fold, cut, baste, and appliqué the center panel. Gently press when completed.

Stitch a large print strip to the left and right side of the center panel.

Stitch a dark blue square to each end of the two remaining large print strips to make a section, and stitch a section to the top and bottom of the center panel to complete the quilt top.

*Scallop Shell and Starfish.*

*Angel Fish and Coral.*

*Crab and Stingray.*

*Turtle and Jellyfish.*

19

# HAWAIIAN CHRISTMAS

## WITH FOUR BLOCKS 48" X 66"

*Hawaiian Christmas.*

## MATERIALS

1⅝ yd. off-white

1⅛ yd. green

½ yd. red

⅝ yd. red/green print

⅛ yd. black

⅜ yd. fabric for binding

54" x 72" piece of thin cotton batting

1½ yd. quilt backing fabric

## CUTTING DIRECTIONS

From the off-white, cut the following:

(2) 19½" x 44" strips—from the strips cut (4) 19½" squares for appliqué backgrounds.

(2) 2½" x 44" strips—keep the strips whole.

(3) 3¼" x 44" strips—from the strips cut a total of (16) 3¼" x 6½" rectangles. Place the rectangles so that half of them are right side up and half are right side down. Cut each rectangle in half diagonally into triangles for a total of (32) triangles.

From the green, cut the following:

(2) 14" x 44" strips—from the strips cut (4) 14" squares for the appliqués.

(3) 3¼" x 44" strips—from the strips cut a total of (16) 3¼" x 6½" rectangles. Place the rectangles so that half of them are right side up and half are right side down. Cut each rectangle in half diagonally into triangles for a total of (32) triangles.

From the red, cut the following:

(7) 2½" x 44" strips—keep (6) of the strips whole and cut the remaining strip into (4) 2½" x 7¼" segments.

From the print, cut the following:

(6) 3½" x 44" strips—keep (4) of the strips whole and cut (2) strips in half.

From the black, cut the following:

(1) 1¼" x 44" strip—keep the strip whole.

From the binding fabric, cut (6) 2" x 44" strips.

## SEWING DIRECTIONS

Refer to the Pattern Section for directions to fold, cut, baste, and appliqué the center panel. Gently press when completed.

Stitch a 4" x 20½" print strip to the left and right sides of the center panel. Stitch a 4" dark green square to each end of the two remaining 4" x 20½" strips and stitch these to the top and bottom of the center panel.

Stitch each hot pink strip to a yellow strip to make a section. Rotary cut across each section in 2" intervals to make a total of (36) cross sections. Stitch the cross sections together into (4) groups of (9) cross sections each.

Line up the groups so that the yellow end is on the left side of each group. Stitch a 1½" x 27½" light green strip to the top of each group and a 1½" x 27½" turquoise strip to the bottom of each group to form (4) identical segments.

Stitch a segment to the left and right sides of the print inner borders. Stitch a 4" dark green square to each end of the two remaining segments and stitch these to the top and bottom of the print inner borders.

Stitch a 4" x 34½" print strip to the left and right sides of the segments. Stitch a 4" dark green square to each end of the two remaining print strips and stitch these strips to the top and bottom of the segments to complete the pieced area.

Baste and appliqué each hibiscus center onto the hibiscus. Fold the off-white border strip in half to find the center. Place a hibiscus flower at the center, 2" from the bottom edge and 1" from the top edge, and pin in place. Place the ends of the dark green border appliqués slightly under the hibiscus 1¼" from the bottom edge. Add two additional green border appliqués and cross the ends. Center the turquoise tulip appliqués above the crossed green borders 1¾" from the top. Place the light green flowers at each end of the strip 1¾" from the top and 1" from the side edges. After all the appliqués are centered and properly placed, follow the directions in the Pattern Section to baste and appliqué them into place. Repeat to make (4) appliquéd borders.

Place a hibiscus on the 8½" off-white square so that the flower top is pointed toward the corner of the square 2¼" from the corner. Center a dark green border 2¾" from the opposite corner and ¾" from the sides. Follow the directions in the Pattern Section to baste and appliqué them into place. Repeat to make (4) appliquéd corner squares.

Stitch an appliquéd border to the left and right sides of the pieced center. Stitch an appliquéd corner square to each end of the two remaining appliquéd borders and stitch them to the pieced center to complete the quilt top.

*Bell and Angel.*

*Snowman with Scarf and Wreath with Bow.*

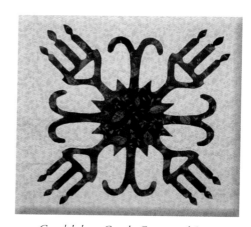

*Candelabra, Candy Cane, and Star.*

*Tree, Gingerbread Man, and Holly Leaf.*

# CHAPTER 2

## TRADITIONAL CENTER- EMBELLISHED WITH ADDED COLORS

This chapter takes the traditional single color block and adds appliqué motifs in additional colors to embellish it. New types of borders both pieced and appliquéd are introduced in this chapter as well. Chapter 2 also explores different quilting styles including a straight line diagonal grid and the traditional Hawaiian method of echo quilting.

# CHRISTMAS CACTUS

### 37" X 37" WALL QUILT

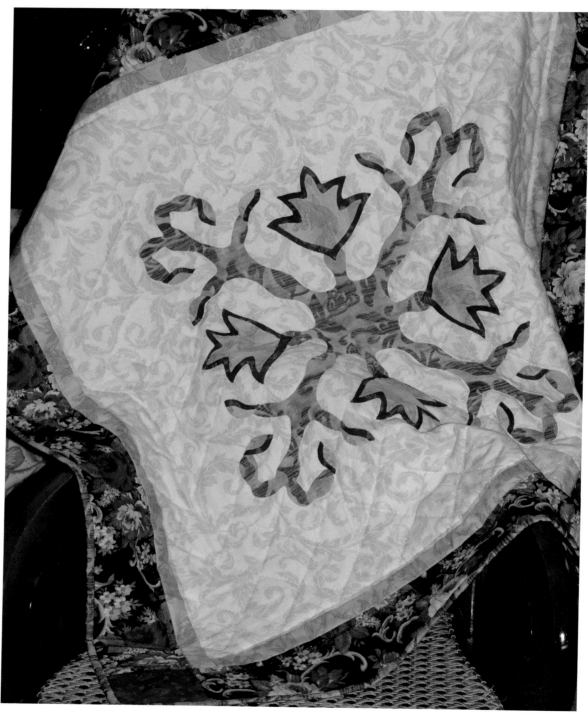

*Christmas Cactus.*

## MATERIALS

⅞ yd. off-white

⅝ yd. green

½ yd. floral print

¼ yd. red

¼ yd. rose

¼ yd. fabric for binding

40" square of thin cotton batting

1⅛ yd. backing fabric

---

## CUTTING DIRECTIONS

From the off-white, cut a 28" x 28" square.

From the green, cut a 20" x 20" square to be used for the appliqué.

From the floral print, cut the following:

    (4) 4" x 44" strips—trim each strip to 4" x 30".

From the red, cut the following:

    (4) 4" squares.

From the rose, cut the following:

    (1) 6" x 32" section—from the section cut (4) 1½" x 32" strips.

Cut the red and rose appliqué pieces as directed in the pattern section. Note that the dotted lines on the red pattern pieces indicate the placement of the corresponding lower case lettered rose pattern pieces.

From the binding fabric, cut (4) 2" x 44" strips.

# SEWING DIRECTIONS

Refer to the Pattern Section for directions to fold, cut, baste, and appliqué the center panel. Gently press when completed.

Stitch a 1½" rose strip to the left and right side of the center panel and trim off ends even with the center. In the same manner, stitch a rose strip to the top and bottom of the center panel.

Stitch a floral print strip to the left and right side of the rose strips.

Stitch a red square to each end of the two remaining floral print strips to make a section, and stitch a section to the top and bottom of the rose strips to complete the quilt top.

The sample quilt follows the general directions to outline quilt the appliqué motifs and accentuate the patchwork by quilting ¼" from the seam line. However, it also contains diagonal lines quilted in both directions through the center panel behind the appliqué to form a decorative grid. This is easily achieved by using a ruler and masking tape to mark straight lines. Place a piece of masking tape from one corner to the opposite one and hand quilt along the tape. Remove the tape and reposition it 2" from the first quilted line. Alternate the directions and continue in this fashion until the grid is complete.

*Christmas Cactus* appliquéd center.

# HIBISCUS AND TULIP BOUQUET

### 57" X 57"

*Hibiscus and Tulip Bouquet.*

## MATERIALS

1⅝ yd. off-white

¾ yd. large floral print

⅝ yd. dark green

½ yd. hot pink

⅜ yd. yellow

¼ yd. turquoise

¼ yd. light green

⅜ yd. fabric for binding

62" square of thin cotton batting

1¾ yd. quilt backing fabric

## CUTTING DIRECTIONS

From the off-white, cut the following:

> (1) 20½" x 44" piece—from the piece cut (1) 20½" x 20½" center background and
> (4) 8½" squares. (4) 8½" x 44" strips—trim the strips to
> (4) 8½" x 41½" strips.

From the floral print, cut the following:

> (6) 4" x 44" strips—cut (2) of the strips in half and trim them to
> (4) 4" x 20½" strips. Trim the remaining strips to (4) 4" x 34½" strips.

From the dark green, cut the following:

> (1) 15" x 15" square for the appliqué.
> (12) 4" squares

From both the hot pink and the yellow, cut the following:

> (4) 2" x 44" strips—keep the strips whole.

From both the turquoise and the light green, cut the following:

> (1) 6" x 27½" strip—cut the strip into (4) 1½" x 27½" strips.

From the binding fabric, cut (6) 2" x 44" strips.

Trace and cut the appliqué pieces of dark green, hot pink, yellow, turquoise, and light green as directed in the Pattern Section.

## SEWING DIRECTIONS

Refer to the Pattern Section for directions to fold, cut, baste, and appliqué the center panel. Gently press when completed.

Stitch a 4" x 20½" print strip to the left and right sides of the center panel. Stitch a 4" dark green square to each end of the two remaining 4" x 20½" strips and stitch these to the top and bottom of the center panel.

*Hibiscus and Tulip Bouquet* appliquéd center.

Stitch each hot pink strip to a yellow strip to make a section. Rotary cut across each section in 2" intervals to make a total of (36) cross sections. Stitch the cross sections together into (4) groups of (9) cross sections each.

Line up the groups so that the yellow end is on the left side of each group. Stitch a 1½" x 27½" light green strip to the top of each group and a 1½" x 27½" turquoise strip to the bottom of each group to form (4) identical segments.

Stitch a segment to the left and right sides of the print inner borders. Stitch a 4" dark green square to each end of the two remaining segments and stitch these to the top and bottom of the print inner borders.

Stitch a 4" x 34½" print strip to the left and right sides of the segments. Stitch a 4" dark green square to each end of the two remaining print strips and stitch these strips to the top and bottom of the segments to complete the pieced area.

Baste and appliqué each hibiscus center onto the hibiscus. Fold the off-white border strip in half to find the center. Place a hibiscus flower at the center, 2" from the bottom edge and 1" from the top edge, and pin in place. Place the ends of the dark green border appliqués slightly under the hibiscus 1¼" from the bottom edge. Add two additional green border appliqués and cross the ends. Center the turquoise tulip appliqués above the crossed green borders 1¾" from the top. Place the light green flowers at each end of the strip 1¾" from the top and 1" from the side edges. After all the appliqués are centered and properly placed, follow the directions in the Pattern Section to baste and appliqué them into place. Repeat to make (4) appliquéd borders.

Place a hibiscus on the 8½" off-white square so that the flower top is pointed toward the corner of the square 2¼" from the corner. Center a dark green border 2¾" from the opposite corner and ¾" from the sides. Follow the directions in the Pattern Section to baste and appliqué them into place. Repeat to make (4) appliquéd corner squares.

Stitch an appliquéd border to the left and right sides of the pieced center. Stitch an appliquéd corner square to each end of the two remaining appliquéd borders and stitch them to the pieced center to complete the quilt top.

# MAY MAZE

30½" X 30½" WALL QUILT

*May Maze.*

# MATERIALS

¾ yd. off-white

½ yd. dark green

¼ yd. each of dark blue, light blue, dark rose, pink, light green, and multi-colored print

¼ yd. fabric for binding

36" square of thin cotton batting

1 yd. backing fabric

---

# CUTTING DIRECTIONS

From the off-white, cut a 26½" x 26½" square.

From the dark green, cut the following:

    (1) 18" x 18" square for the appliqué.

    (2) 2½" squares

From each of the dark blue, light blue, dark rose, pink, light green, and multi print, cut:

    (1) 2½" x 44" strip—keep the strip whole.

Cut the dark green, dark blue, light blue, dark rose, pink, light green, and multi print appliqué pieces as directed in the Pattern Section.

From the binding fabric, cut (3) 2" x 44" strips.

---

# SEWING DIRECTIONS

Refer to the Pattern Section for directions to fold, cut, baste, and stitch the dark green central appliqué in place. Baste and appliqué the light green leaves onto the dark green.

Center each coxcomb center over the coxcomb, baste, and appliqué it in place. In the same manner, appliqué each onion center onto the onion, and each dark blue bottom onto the bluebell.

Using the off-white fold lines as a guide, place the onion top slightly under the onion point and appliqué it into place. Baste and appliqué the remaining coxcombs and bluebells to complete the center panel and lightly press.

Stitch the 2½" strips together by threes into (2) sections—dark blue, pink, light green in one section and light blue, dark rose, and multi in the other section. Rotary cut across each section at 2½" intervals to make (9) cross sections of each section for a total of (18) cross sections.

Stitch together (4) cross sections (two of each type) with (1) dark green square to make a Segment A. Make (2) A Segments. Note that the cross sections may be placed in different directions to achieve an interesting random look. Stitch a Segment A to the left and right sides of the center panel.

Stitch together (5) cross sections in different directions to make a Segment B and make (2) B Segments. Stitch a Segment B to the top and bottom of the center panel to complete the quilt top.

# CHAPTER 3

## EMBELLISHED BLOCK-USED REPEATED TIMES

The quilts in Chapter 3 feature the same block repeated multiple times. The blocks may be identical using the same colors throughout or may appear in different colors. Each of these quilts employs extensive patchwork to enhance and showcase the Hawaiian style blocks.

# BUTTERFLY TRAILS

36½" X 36½" WALL QUILT

*Butterfly Trails.*

## MATERIALS

¾ yd. white

¼ yd. each of maroon, lavender, blue, and pink

⅛ yd. yellow

⅝ yd. butterfly or floral print

¼ yd. fabric for binding

40" square of thin cotton batting

1⅛ yd. backing fabric

---

## CUTTING DIRECTIONS

From the white, cut the following:

(1) 10½" x 44" strip—from the strip cut (4) 10½" squares.

(2) 4" x 44" strips—from one strip cut (4) 4" squares.

From the second strip cut (16) 4" x 2¼" rectangles.

(2) 3⅜" x 44" strips—from the strips cut (20) 3⅜" squares. Cut each square in half diagonally into right triangles for a total of (40) triangles.

From each of the maroon, lavender, blue, and pink, cut the following:

(1) 9" square for the appliqué. Follow the directions in the Pattern Section to cut a butterfly trail appliqué piece for each color.

(4) 3⅜" squares—cut each square in half diagonally into right triangles for a total of (8) triangles.

(1) 2" square

(3) butterfly appliqués

From the yellow, cut the following:

(4) 3⅜" squares—cut each square in half diagonally into right triangles for a total of (8) triangles.

(1) 2" square

(4) butterfly appliqués

From the print, cut the following:

(4) 3" x 44" strips—keep the strips whole.

(3) 2" x 44" strips—cut one strip into (4) 2" x 10½" strips. Cut each of the remaining strips in half into (4) 2" by 22" strips.

From the binding fabric, cut (4) 2" x 44" strips.

*Butterfly Trails* appliquéd block.

## SEWING DIRECTIONS

Refer to the Pattern Section for directions to fold, cut, baste, and appliqué the four butterfly trail blocks. After the trail appliqués are stitched, center and baste the butterfly appliqués onto them. The maroon trail has (clockwise) pink, blue, yellow, and lavender butterflies. The lavender trail has blue, yellow, pink, and maroon. The blue trail has lavender, pink, maroon, and yellow. The pink trail has yellow, maroon, lavender, and blue. Press each block.

Stitch a 2" x 10½" print strip between the maroon and lavender trail blocks to form the upper center section. Stitch another 2" x 10½" strip between the blue and pink trail blocks to form the lower center section. Stitch a yellow square between the remaining 2" x 10½" print strips to form a sashing section. Stitch the sashing section between the upper and lower sections.

Stitch a 2" x 22" strip to the left and right sides of the center. Stitch a pink and blue square to the ends of the third 2" x 22" strip and a lavender and maroon square to the ends of the fourth strip. Stitch the third strip to the top of the center and the fourth strip to the bottom of the center.

To form a pieced butterfly, stitch a white triangle to a colored triangle along adjacent short sides to form a large triangle. Stitch two large triangles together to form a 4" square butterfly block. Make (4) butterfly blocks each in pink, lavender, yellow, maroon, and blue and keep them in this order. Stitch a 2¼" x 4" white rectangle between each color butterfly block to make a butterfly border, and make (4) butterfly borders.

Stitch a butterfly border to the left and right sides of the center. Stitch a 4" white square to each end of the remaining two butterfly borders, and stitch these to the top and bottom of the center. Note that the butterfly border seams are pressed toward the print borders, and all other seams are pressed open.

Stitch a 3" x 44" print strip to the left and right sides of the butterfly borders and trim off the strip ends even with the butterfly borders. In the same manner, stitch the remaining 3" x 44" print strips to the top and bottom butterfly borders and trim off the ends to complete the quilt top.

# FOUR COLOR TULIPS

43" X 43"

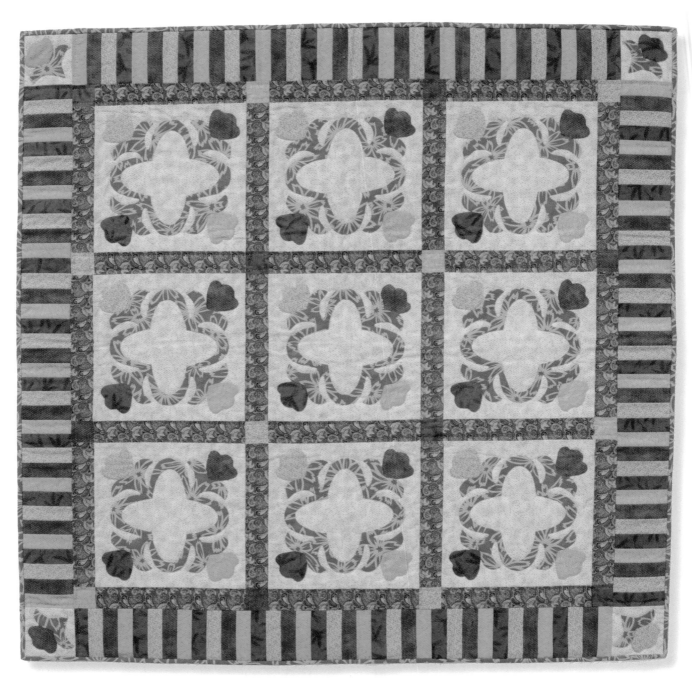

*Four Color Tulips.*

## MATERIALS

1 yd. off-white

¾ yd. green

⅜ yd. multicolored print

⅜ yd. each of light blue, dark blue, maroon, and pink

⅜ yd. fabric for binding

45" square of thin cotton batting

1¼ yd. backing fabric

## CUTTING DIRECTIONS

From the off-white, cut the following:

> (3) 10½" x 44" strips—from the strips cut a total of (9) 10½" squares and (4) 4" squares.

From the green, cut the following:

> (3) 9" x 44" strips—from the strips cut a total of (9) 9" squares for the center appliqués and remaining fabric for the corner appliqués.

From the print, cut the following:

> (6) 2" x 44" strips—from each strip cut (4) 2" x 10½" segments for a total of (24) segments.

From each of the light blue, dark blue, maroon, and pink, cut the following:

> (1) 2" x 44" strip—from the strip cut (4) 2" squares. Trim the remainder of the strip to 1½".
>
> (3) 1½" x 44" strips—keep the strips whole.

Cut the colored appliqués as directed in the Pattern Section.

From the binding fabric, cut (5) 2" x 44" strips.

*Four Color Tulips* appliquéd block.

## SEWING DIRECTIONS

Refer to the Pattern Section for directions to fold, cut, baste, and appliqué the squares. Slip the tulip appliqués slightly under the green and always keep the same clockwise color order of pink, dark blue, light blue, and maroon. Each square is identical. For the corner squares, center the appliqué diagonally on the 4" off-white square and make one of each color tulip.

Line up the central blocks in (3) horizontal rows of (3) blocks each. Be sure that the colored tulips are all in the same position. Stitch a print segment between each of the blocks and on the outer left and right sides of each horizontal row to make a section.

Make (4) horizontal rows of (4) 2" colored squares and (3) print segments each, placing the colored squares in the following order:

> Row 1: dark blue, light blue, maroon, pink
>
> Row 2: pink, dark blue, light blue, maroon
>
> Row 3: maroon, pink, dark blue, light blue
>
> Row 4: light blue, maroon, pink, dark blue

Stitch rows 2 and 3 between the (3) horizontal sections, row 1 on the top, and row 4 on the bottom.

Stitch together four of the same length 1½" strips (one of each color) to make a border section in the following order: dark blue, light blue, maroon, and pink. Rotary cut across each border section at 4" intervals to make a total of (36) cross sections. Stitch together (9) cross sections in the same order to make a border segment. Make a total of (4) border segments.

Stitch a border segment to the left and right sides of the print rows starting with the dark blue end. Stitch an appliquéd corner square to each end of the two remaining border segments. Stitch one of these to the top and one to the bottom to complete the quilt top.

# TAHITIAN DREAM

70" X 98"—TWIN/FULL SIZE

*Tahitian Dream.*

## MATERIALS

2 yd. black

1⅞ yd. pale yellow

1½ yd. white

⅞ yd. large tropical print

¾ yd. each of orange and turquoise

½ yd. each of red and lavender

⅝ yd. fabric for binding

Full size thin cotton batting

2½ yd. quilt backing fabric

## CUTTING DIRECTIONS

From the black, cut the following:

(16) 4⅜" x 44" strips—from the strips cut (140) 4⅜" squares. Cut each square in half diagonally into right triangles for a total of (280) triangles.

From the pale yellow, cut the following:

(7) 4" x 44" strips—from the strips cut (68) 4" squares.

(8) 4⅜" x 44" strips—from the strips cut (68) 4⅜" squares. Cut each square in half diagonally into right triangles for a total of (136) triangles.

From the white, cut the following:

(5) 10¼" x 44" strips—from the strips cut (18) 10¼" squares.

From the tropical print, cut the following:

(4) 7½" x 44" strips—from the strips cut (17) 7½" squares.

From each of the orange, red, lavender, and turquoise, cut the following:

(2) 4" x 44" strips—from the strips cut (18) 4" squares.

Follow the directions in the Pattern Section to cut (5) each of the orange and turquoise appliqués and (4) each of the red and lavender appliqués.

From the binding fabric, cut (10) 2" x 44" strips.

## SEWING DIRECTIONS

Follow the directions in the Pattern Section to cut, baste, and appliqué (18) white squares, (5) orange, (5) turquoise, (4) red, and (4) lavender. Thoroughly press each square.

The quilt is composed of two different blocks, A and B. There are (18) A blocks and (17) B blocks.

Block A contains the following:

(1) appliquéd white square

(8) black triangles

(4) colored squares (1 each of turquoise, lavender, red, and orange)

**To Make Block A**, stitch a black triangle to two adjoining sides of a colored square to form a large triangle. Stitch a large triangle to each side of the appliquéd white square, opposite sides, then remaining opposite sides. Use the illustration for placement of the corner colored squares. Each A block has the same colored square placement.

Block B contains the following:

(1) tropical print square

(8) black triangles

(8) pale yellow triangles

(4) pale yellow squares

**To Make Block B**, stitch each black triangle to a pale yellow triangle to make a square. Make (8) black/yellow squares. Stitch together (2) of the squares with the black sides facing each other to make a rectangle and make (4) rectangles. Stitch a rectangle to each side of the tropical print square. Stitch a yellow square to each end of the remaining rectangles to make a section. Stitch a section to the top and bottom to complete the block.

The quilt is composed of (7) horizontal rows of (5) blocks each. Rows 1, 3, 5, and 7 begin and end with an A block alternating with two B blocks. Rows 2, 4, and 6 begin and end with a B block alternating with two A blocks. The position of the colored appliquéd centers is as follows:

Row 1: orange, turquoise, lavender

Row 2: red, orange

Row 3: turquoise, lavender, red

Row 4: orange, turquoise

Row 5: lavender, red, orange

Row 6: turquoise, lavender

Row 7: red, orange, turquoise

Stitch the horizontal rows together to complete the quilt top.

(4) colored squares (1 each of turquoise, lavender, red, and orange)

*Tahitian Dream* close-up.

40

# CHAPTER
# 4

# EMBELLISHED
# BLOCK-CENTER MEDALLION
# WITH PATCHWORK

The three quilts in this chapter are vastly similar in construction,
yet have very different focal points. The similarities are easily apparent. Each has a
multicolor appliquéd center surrounded by a large floral inner border and additional solid
color border to accentuate the appliqué work. Each uses two different 12" blocks,
one a star, and has basically the same outer border.

Very slight changes in the blocks and placement of colors, however, render the
designs quite different in appearance. The *Exotic Purple Lily* features framed blocks with
the floral print incorporated into the background. The *Amazing Amaryllis* reveals striking
crisscrossed diagonal lines with the floral print as a featured motif.
The *Daffodils and Bluebirds* design provides dual focus between the floral
print enhanced stars and the patchwork daffodils.

Although the star blocks are placed in exactly the same location for all three
quilts, they are recognizable as stars in only one of them. The subtle differences
make each design pleasing and unique. All of the quilts in
Chapter 4 quilts have been photographed on a large flat surface
so they may be viewed in their entirety.

# EXOTIC PURPLE LILY

66" X 90"—TWIN SIZE

*Exotic Purple Lily.*

# MATERIALS

1¾ yd. lavender

1½ yd. yellow

1¼ yd. large tropical print

1 yd. black

⅞ yd. white

½ yd. turquoise

⅜ yd. dark purple

½ yd. dark green

⅛ yd. or scraps of light green

½ yd. fabric for binding

Twin size thin cotton batting

2 yd. quilt backing fabric

---

# CUTTING DIRECTIONS

From the lavender, cut the following:

(5) 5¼" x 44" strips—from the strips cut (35) 5¼" squares. Cut each square in half diagonally into right triangles for a total of (70) large triangles.

(8) 3⅞" x 44" strips—from the strips cut (72) 3⅞" squares. Cut each square in half diagonally into right triangles for a total of (144) triangles.

From the yellow, cut the following:

(9) 3½ "x 44" strips—from the strips cut the following segments:

(6) 3½" x 18½"

(8) 3½" x 15½"

(8) 3½" x 12½"

(4) 3⅞" x 44" strips—from the strips cut (38) 3⅞" squares. Cut each square in half diagonally into right triangles for a total of (76) triangles.

From the large tropical print, cut the following:

(4) 4½" x 44" strips—keep the strips whole.

(6) 3⅞" x 44" strips—from the strips cut (56) 3⅞" squares. Cut each square in half diagonally into right triangles for a total of (112) triangles.

From the black, cut the following:

(3) 5¼" x 44" strips—from the strips cut (24) 5¼" squares. Cut each square in half diagonally into right triangles for a total of (48) large triangles.

(3) 3⅞" x 44" strips—from the strips cut (24) 3⅞" squares. Cut each square in half diagonally into right triangles for a total of (48) small triangles.

(1) 3½" x 44" strip—from the strip cut (8) 3½" squares.

From the white, cut the following:

(1) 22½" x 44" strip—from the strip cut (1) 22½" square—from the remainder of the strip cut (9) 6½" squares.

(1) 6½" x 44" strip—from the strip cut (5) 6½" squares and add to the (9) squares for a total of (14) 6 ½" squares.

From the turquoise, cut the following:

(5) 3½" x 44" strips—from the strips cut (56) 3½" squares.

From the purple, cut the following:

(2) 4⅞" x 44" strips—from the strips cut (12) 4⅞" squares.

From the binding fabric, cut (8) 2" x 44" strips.

Trace and cut the dark green, light green, lavender, purple, and yellow appliqué pieces as directed in the Pattern Section.

---

## SEWING DIRECTIONS

In addition to the appliquéd center, the quilt is composed of two different pieced blocks, A and B. There are (14) A blocks and (12) B blocks.

Block A contains the following:

(1) white square

(4) large lavender triangles

(8) tropical print triangles

(4) turquoise squares

**To Make Block A**, stitch (2) tropical print triangles to each large lavender triangle to form a rectangle. Stitch a rectangle to each side of the white square center. Stitch a turquoise square to each end of the remaining rectangles to make a section. Stitch a section to the top and bottom to complete the block. Make a total of (14) A blocks.

Block B contains the following:

(1) purple square

(4) yellow triangles

(4) large black triangles

(12) lavender triangles

(4) small black triangles

**To Make Block B**, stitch (4) yellow triangles to the purple square, opposite sides first, then remaining opposite sides, to form a center square. Stitch (2) lavender triangles to each large black triangle to make a rectangle, and stitch a rectangle to each side of the center square. Stitch (4) lavender triangles to (4) small black triangles to form squares. Stitch a lavender/black square to each end of the remaining rectangles to make a section. Stitch a section to the top and bottom to complete the block. Make a total of (12) B blocks.

Carefully press the completed appliquéd center to remove the fold lines. Manipulate the tropical print strips to achieve a flowing arrangement. Stitch a strip to each side of the center and trim off the strip ends even with the center. In the same manner, stitch the remaining tropical print strips to the top and bottom, trimming off the strip ends.

Stitch a yellow triangle to each side of a large lavender triangle to form a rectangle. Repeat for each remaining large lavender triangle to form a total of (14) rectangles. Set aside (10) of the rectangles for the outer border.

Stitch a lavender/yellow rectangle between (2) 3½" x 12½" yellow segments to form an inner border section. Make a total of (4) inner border sections, and stitch one to the left and right side of the center. Stitch a black square to each end of the two remaining border sections and stitch these to the top and bottom to complete the center medallion.

Stitch a B block between two A blocks to form a vertical row and stitch the row to the right side of the center medallion. Repeat to form another vertical row and stitch it to the left side of the center medallion.

Stitch a (5) block horizontal row alternating A and B blocks beginning and ending with an A block. In the same manner stitch a horizontal row beginning and ending with a B block. Stitch these rows together to form an A/B section. Pin and stitch the section to the top of the quilt.

Make an additional A/B section. Pin and stitch the second section to the bottom of the quilt.

Using the yellow segments and lavender/yellow rectangles, stitch together the following to make a side outer border. Make a total of two side borders and pin and stitch one to each side.

15½" segment, rectangle, 18½" segment, rectangle, 18½" segment, rectangle, 15½" segment

Using the yellow segments and lavender/yellow rectangles, stitch together the following to make the top and bottom outer borders.

15½" segment, rectangle, 18½" segment, rectangle, 15½" segment

Stitch a black square to each end of the top and bottom outer borders. Pin and stitch these in place to complete the quilt top.

*Exotic Purple Lily* appliquéd center.

Patchwork detail of *Exotic Purple Lily*.

# AMAZING AMARYLLIS

66" X 90"—TWIN SIZE

*Amazing Amaryllis.*

# MATERIALS

1⅜ yd. white

1¼ yd. black

1⅛ yd. deep hot pink

1 yd. large tropical print

1 yd. dark green

⅝ yd. light pink

⅝ yd. tan

⅜ yd. lavender

⅛ yd. or scraps of light green

½ yd. fabric for binding

Twin size thin cotton batting

2 yd. quilt backing fabric

---

# CUTTING DIRECTIONS

From the white, cut the following:

(1) 22½" x 44" strip—from the strip cut (1) 22½" square—from the remainder of the strip cut (12) 5¼" squares.

(2) 5¼" x 44" strips—from the strips cut (16) 5¼" squares for a total of (28) 5¼" squares. Cut each square in half diagonally into right triangles for a total of (56) large triangles.

(3) 3⅞" x 44" strips—from the strips cut (24) 3⅞" squares. Cut each square in half diagonally into right triangles for a total of (48) small triangles.

From the black, cut the following:

(11) 3⅞" x 44" strips—from the strips cut (110) 3⅞" squares. Cut each square in half diagonally into right triangles for a total of (220) triangles.

From the deep hot pink, cut the following:

(1) 3⅞" x 44" strip—from the strip cut (2) 3⅞" squares. Cut each square in half diagonally into right triangles for a total of (4) triangles. Trim the remainder of the strip to 3½" x 30½".

(10) 3½" x 44" strips—keep (6) of the strips whole, cut (1) of the strips in half, and trim the remaining (3) strips to 3½" x 30½".

From the tropical print, cut the following:

(4) 4½" x 44" strips

(2) 6½" x 44" strips—from the strips cut (12) 6½" squares.

From the dark green, cut the following:

(5) 3½" x 44" strips—from each strip cut (12) 3½" squares for a total of (60) squares.

From the light pink, cut the following:

(3) 5¼" x 44" strips—from the strips cut (24) 5¼" squares. Cut each square in half diagonally into right triangles for a total of (48) large triangles.

From the tan, cut the following:

    (5) 3⅞" x 44" strips—from the strips cut (48) 3⅞" squares. Cut each square in half diagonally into right triangles for a total of (96) triangles.

From the lavender, cut the following:

    (2) 4⅞" x 44" strips—from the strips cut (14) 4⅞" squares.

From the binding fabric, cut (8) 2" x 44" strips.

The light green is for the appliqué only. Trace and cut the dark green, light green, hot pink, light pink, and lavender appliqué pieces as directed in the Pattern Section.

---

## SEWING DIRECTIONS

In addition to the appliquéd center, the quilt is composed of two different pieced blocks, A and B. There are (14) A blocks and (12) B blocks.

Block A contains the following:

    (1) lavender square

    (12) black triangles

    (4) large white triangles

    (4) dark green squares

**To Make Block A**, stitch (4) black triangles to the lavender square, opposite sides first then remaining opposite sides, to form a center square. Stitch (2) black triangles to each large white triangle to make a rectangle, and stitch a rectangle to each side of the center square. Stitch a green square to each end of the remaining rectangles to make a section. Stitch a section to the top and bottom to complete the block. Make a total of (14) A blocks.

Block B contains the following:

    (1) tropical print square

    (4) large light pink triangles

    (8) tan triangles

    (4) black triangles

    (4) small white triangles

**To Make Block B**, stitch (2) tan triangles to each light pink triangle to make a rectangle. Stitch a rectangle to each side of the tropical print square. Stitch each black triangle to a small white triangle to make a square. Stitch a black/white square to each end of the remaining rectangles, with the white side next to the tan, to make a section. Stitch a section to the top and bottom to complete the block. Make a total of (12) B blocks.

Carefully press the completed appliquéd center to remove the fold lines. Manipulate the tropical print strips to achieve a pleasing arrangement. Stitch a strip to each side of the center and trim off the strip ends even with the center. In the same manner, stitch the remaining strips to the top and bottom, trimming off the strip ends.

Stitch a 3½" x 30½" deep hot pink strip to each side of the center. Stitch (4) hot pink triangles to (4) black triangles to make (4) squares. Stitch a hot pink/black square to each end of the remaining 3½" x 30½" hot pink strips with the hot pink half next to the strip end. Stitch these strips to the top and bottom to complete the center medallion.

Stitch a B block between two A blocks to form a vertical row and stitch the row to one side of the center medallion. Repeat to form another vertical row and stitch it to the other side of the center medallion.

Stitch a (5) block horizontal row alternating A and B blocks beginning and ending with an A block. In the same manner stitch a horizontal row beginning and ending with a B block. Stitch these rows together to form an A/B section. Pin and stitch the section to the top of the quilt.

Make an additional A/B section. Pin and stitch the second section to the bottom of the quilt.

Stitch (4) whole deep hot pink strips together by twos and each of the remaining (2) whole strips to a half strip to form the outer borders. Stitch a long strip to each side and trim off the edges even with the blocks. Trim the short strips to 60½" and stitch a dark green square to each end. Stitch the short strips to the top and bottom of the quilt.

*Amazing Amaryllis* appliquéd center.

Two patchwork blocks of *Amazing Amaryllis*.

# DAFFODILS AND BLUEBIRDS

66" X 90"—TWIN SIZE

*Daffodils and Bluebirds.*

# MATERIALS

1⅝ yd. yellow

1⅜ yd. peach

1⅜ yd. dark green

⅞ yd. light green

⅞ yd. large tropical print

¾ yd. white

¼ yd. or scraps of blue

½ yd. fabric for binding

Twin size thin cotton batting

2 yd. quilt backing fabric

---

# CUTTING DIRECTIONS

From the yellow, cut the following:

(8) 3½" x 44" strips—from the strips cut (48) 3½" x 6½" rectangles.

(5) 5¼" x 44" strips—from the strips cut (35) 5¼" squares. Cut each square in half diagonally into right triangles for a total of (70) large triangles.

From the peach, cut the following:

(9) 3½" x 44" strips—from the strips cut the following segments:

(6) 3½" x 18½"

(8) 3½" x 15½"

(8) 3½" x 12½"

From the remaining ends, cut (4) 3½" squares.

(2) 4⅞" x 44" strips—from one strip cut (8) 4⅞" squares and from the second strip cut (4) 4⅞" squares for a total of (12) 4⅞" squares.

Trim the remainder of the second strip to 3⅞" and cut (6) 3⅞" squares. Cut each of the 3⅞" squares in half diagonally into right triangles for a total of (12) triangles.

(1) 3⅞" x 44" strip—from the strip cut (10) 3⅞" squares. Cut each square in half diagonally into right triangles for a total of (20) triangles. Add these to the (12) triangles for a total of (32) triangles.

From the dark green, cut the following:

(8) 3⅞" x 44" strips—from the strips cut (80) 3⅞" squares. Cut each square in half diagonally into right triangles for a total of (160) triangles.

From the light green, cut the following:

(5) 3½" x 44" strips—from the strips cut (56) 3½" squares.

(3) 3⅞" x 44" strips—from the strips cut (26) 3⅞" squares. Cut each square in half diagonally into right triangles for a total of (52) triangles.

From the tropical print, cut the following:

(4) 4½" x 44" strips—keep the strips whole.

(3) 6½" x 44" strips—from the strips cut (14) 6½" squares.

From the white, cut the following:

    (1) 22½" x 44" strip—from the strip cut (1) 22½" square.

From the remainder of the strip cut (5) 3⅞" x 21" segments.

Cut each segment into (5) 3⅞" squares for a total of (24) squares. Cut each square in half diagonally into right triangles for a total of (48) triangles.

From the binding fabric, cut (8) 2" x 44" strips.

The blue is for the appliqué only. Trace and cut the dark green, blue, yellow, and peach appliqué pieces as directed in the Pattern Section.

---

## SEWING DIRECTIONS

In addition to the appliquéd center, the quilt is composed of two different pieced blocks, A and B. There are (14) A blocks and (12) B blocks.

Block A contains the following:

    (1) tropical print square

    (4) large yellow triangles

    (8) dark green triangles

    (4) light green squares

**To Make Block A**, stitch (2) dark green triangles to each large yellow triangle to make a rectangle. Stitch a rectangle to each side of the tropical print square. Stitch a light green square to each end of the remaining (2) rectangles to make a section. Stitch a section to the top and bottom to complete the block. Make a total of (14) A blocks.

Block B contains the following:

    (1) peach square

    (4) white triangles

    (4) yellow rectangles

    (4) dark green triangles

    (4) light green triangles

**To Make Block B**, stitch (4) white triangles to the peach square, opposite sides first, then remaining opposite sides, to form a center square. Stitch a yellow rectangle to each side of the center square. Stitch each dark green triangle to a light green triangle to make a square. Stitch a dark green/light green square to each end of the remaining two yellow rectangles to make a section. Place the dark green side next to the yellow. Stitch a section to the top and bottom to complete the block. Make a total of (12) B blocks.

Carefully press the completed appliquéd center to remove the fold lines. Manipulate the tropical print strips to achieve a flowing arrangement. Stitch a strip to each side of the center and trim off the strip ends even with the center. In the same manner, stitch the remaining tropical print strips to the top and bottom, trimming off the strip ends.

Stitch a peach triangle to each side of a large yellow triangle to form a rectangle. Repeat to form a total of (14) rectangles. Set aside (10) of the rectangles for the outer border.

Stitch a yellow/peach rectangle between (2) 3½" x 12½" peach segments to form an inner border section. Make a total of (4) inner border sections, and stitch one to the left and right side of the center. Stitch (4) peach triangles to (4) light green triangles to make (4) squares. Stitch a peach/light green square to each end of the two remaining border sections with the peach half next to the strip end. Stitch these to the top and bottom to complete the center medallion.

Stitch a B block between two A blocks to form a vertical row and stitch the row to the right side of the center medallion. Repeat to form another vertical row and stitch it to the left side of the center medallion.

Stitch a (5) block horizontal row alternating A and B blocks beginning and ending with an A block. In the same manner stitch a horizontal row beginning and ending with a B block. Stitch these rows together to form an A/B section. Pin and stitch the section to the top of the quilt.

Make an additional A/B section. Pin and stitch the second section to the bottom of the quilt.

Using the peach segments and yellow/peach rectangles, stitch together the following to make a side outer border. Make a total of two side borders and pin and stitch one to each side.

15½" segment, rectangle, 18½" segment, rectangle, 18½" segment, rectangle, 15½" segment

Using the peach segments and yellow/peach rectangles, stitch together the following to make the top and bottom outer borders.

15½" segment, rectangle, 18½" segment, rectangle, 15½" segment

Stitch a peach square to each end of the top and bottom outer borders. Pin and stitch these in place to complete the quilt top.

*Daffodils and Bluebirds* appliquéd center.

Two patchwork blocks of *Daffodils and Bluebirds*.

# CHAPTER 5

## PATTERNS

### Directions for Cutting and Stitching Hand-Appliquéd Hawaiian Blocks

The traditional cutting method is to pin the pattern onto the fabric that has been folded in eighths and cut through all eight layers at once using small sharp scissors. I find that this method can cause some distortion and irregularity in the appliqué, and I offer the following procedure instead.

Photocopy or trace the appliqué pattern from the book and cut it out using paper scissors. Trace the pattern onto a manila folder or other template material and cut it out.

Thoroughly press both the appliqué and background fabrics. Fold each in half, then in quarters, and each quarter in half diagonally into eighths. Either finger press or iron the folds. Each fold will intersect the center of the fabric.

Place the appliqué fabric right side down on a flat surface. Lay the manila pattern on the wrong side of the fabric along the fold lines with the pattern point at the center of the fabric. The longer line of the pattern goes along the diagonal or bias fold. Using a fine point pen, trace along the curved edges of the pattern but not the fold lines. Turn the pattern piece over as you move from one fold to the next until the appliqué design is complete.

Cut out the appliqué along the traced lines. Center the appliqué right side up on the background fabric, matching the folded lines, and pin in place.

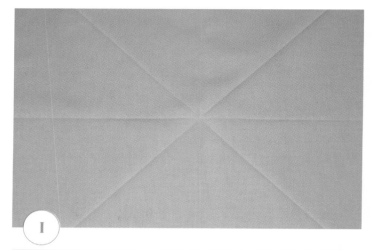

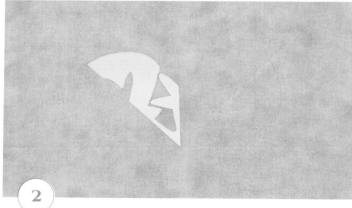

Carefully baste the appliqué to the background ¼" from the outer and inner edges. Use great care with this step to ensure that the appliqué lies flat and is properly aligned. The sample uses black basting thread to allow better visibility.

With fine quality matching thread, stitch the appliqué to the background using the needle turn appliqué method. Tuck under approximately ⅛" of the raw edge to the basting line and catch one or two threads of the appliqué to make the stitch nearly invisible. Remove the basting thread after the appliqué is fully stitched, and carefully press on the wrong side of the background.

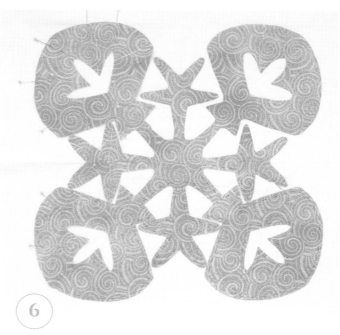

# Directions for Cutting and Stitching Machine-Appliquéd Hawaiian Blocks

Follow the same steps to photocopy the pattern, transfer it onto the manila folder, and cut it out. Press both the appliqué and background fabrics.

Cut an 18" square piece of lightweight fusible web and iron it onto the back of the appliqué fabric. Fold both the appliqué and background fabrics in quarters only.

Follow the directions above to trace the appliqué design onto the paper side of the fusible web which has been ironed onto the wrong side of the appliqué fabric. Cut it out slightly inside the traced lines. Remove the paper backing.

Center the appliqué on the background fabric, matching the fold lines of each, and iron it into place. There is no need to pin or baste, as the appliqué is firmly attached to the background.

Cut an 18" square piece of lightweight fusible interfacing for a stabilizer and iron it onto the wrong side of the background fabric, covering the area of the appliqué.

Set the sewing machine for a medium width zigzag stitch. Using thread to match the appliqué, finish the inner and outer edges with stitching.

Press from the wrong side of the background.

The photos below show a comparison between the hand and machine-appliquéd versions of the Scallop Shell and Starfish block featured in Chapter 1. The edges can be further trimmed on the machine-appliquéd version to make it appear more like the hand-appliquéd one.

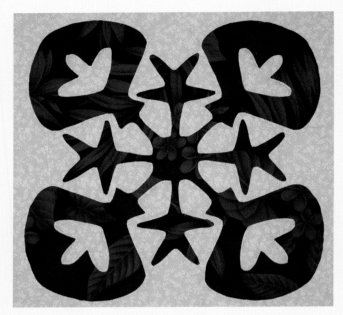

Hand appliquéd version of the *Scallop Shell and Starfish* block.

Machine appliquéd version of the *Scallop Shell and Starfish* block

# HAWAIIAN SEAS
## Angel Fish and Coral

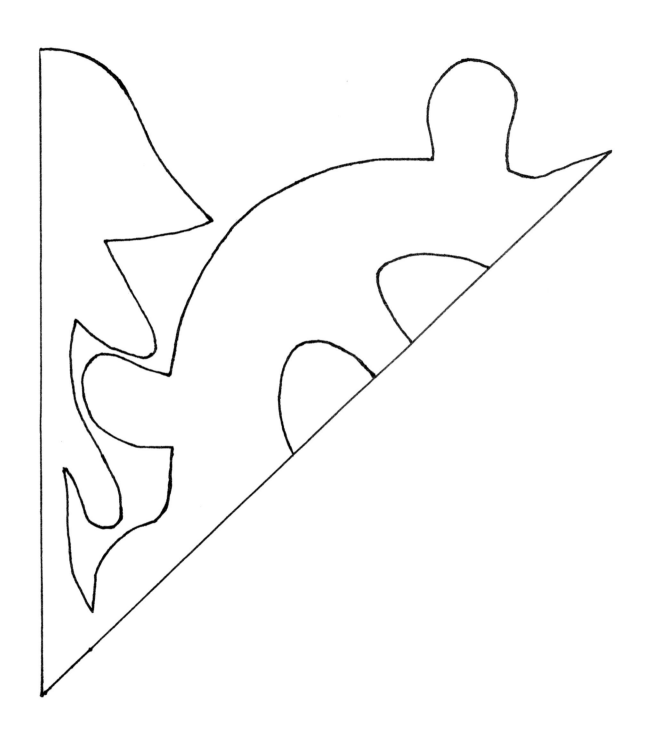

# HAWAIIAN CHRISTMAS
## Bell and Angel

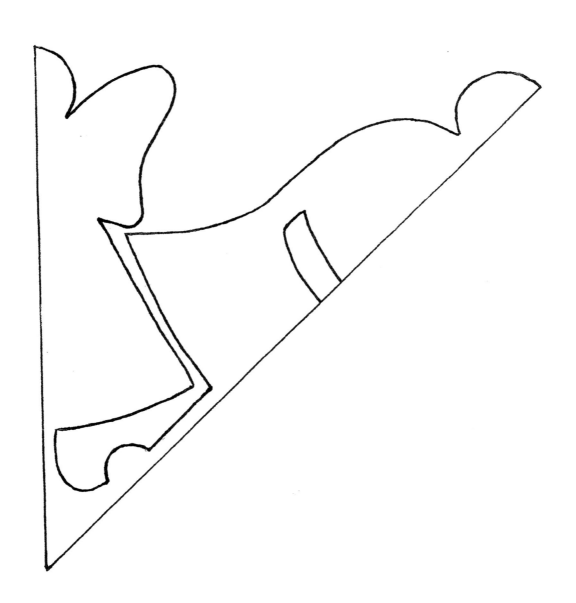

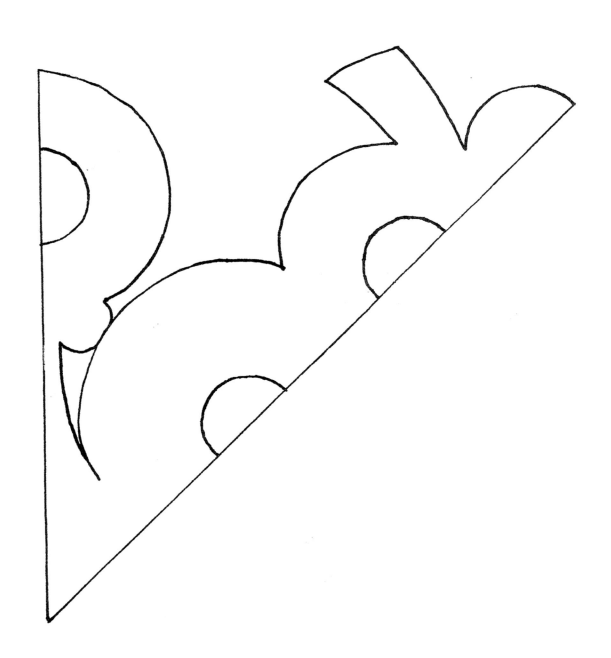

# HAWAIIAN CHRISTMAS
## Candelabra, Candy Cane, and Star

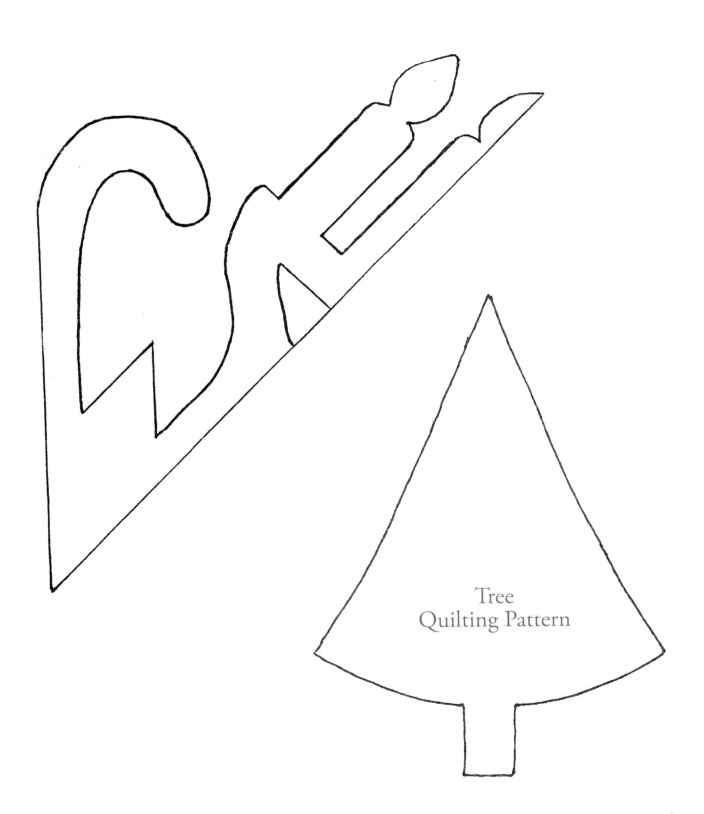

Tree
Quilting Pattern

# HAWAIIAN CHRISTMAS
Tree, Gingerbread Man,
and Holly Leaf

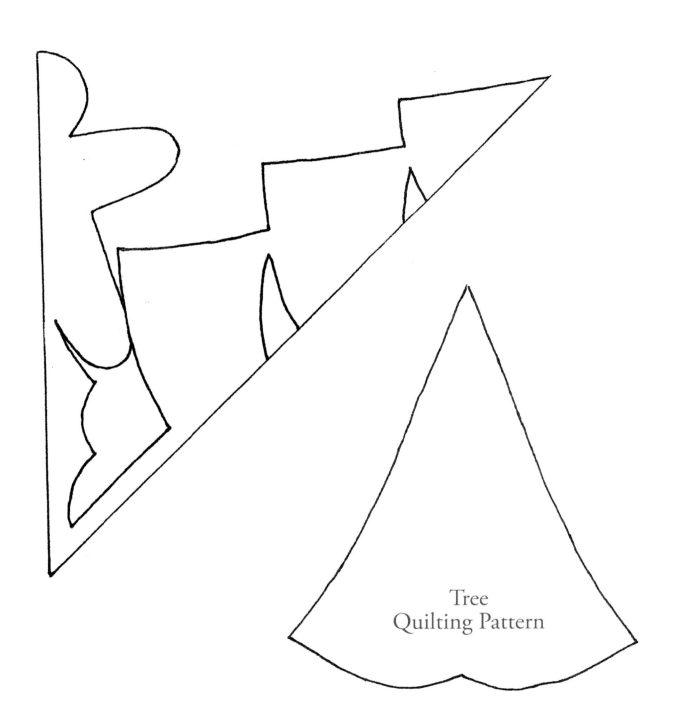

Tree
Quilting Pattern

# CHRISTMAS CACTUS

d
rose CUT 4

b
rose CUT 4

e
rose CUT 4

D
Red CUT 4

B
Red CUT 4

E
Red CUT 4

C
Red CUT 4

a
rose CUT 4

c
Rose CUT 4

Green

A
Red CUT 4

# HIBISCUS AND TULIP BOUQUET

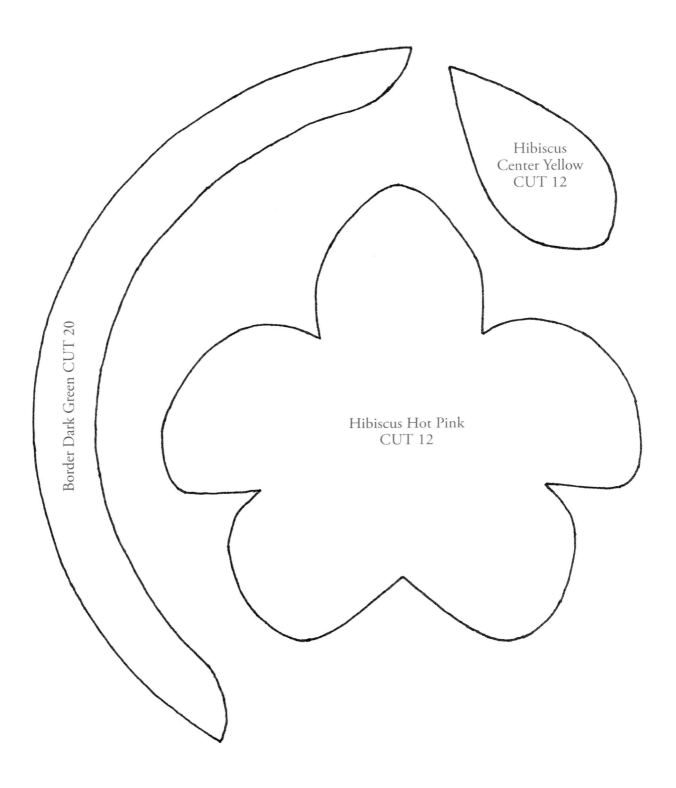

Hibiscus
Center Yellow
CUT 12

Hibiscus Hot Pink
CUT 12

Border Dark Green CUT 20

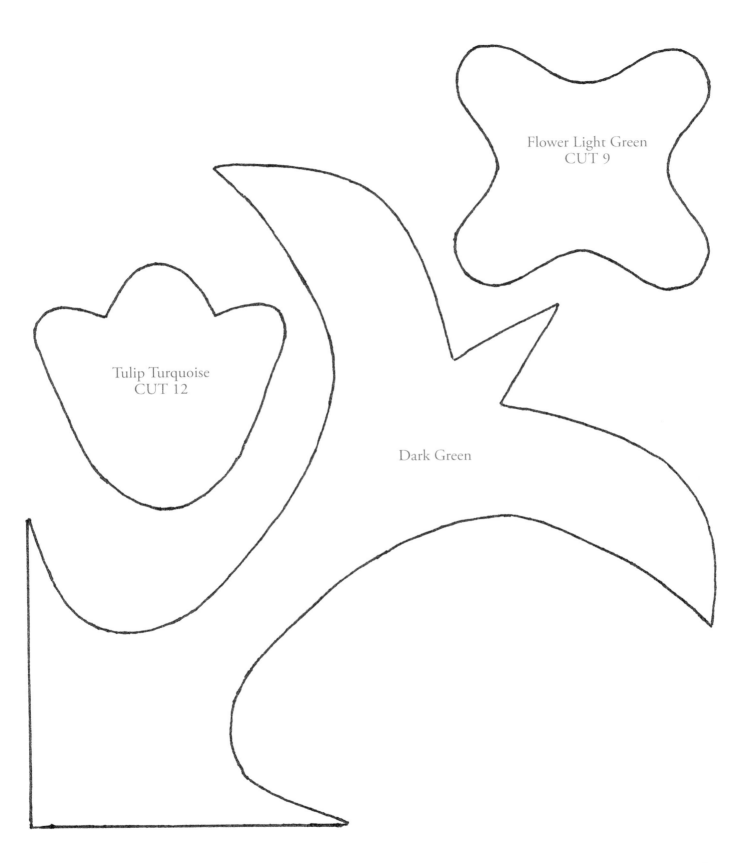

Flower Light Green
CUT 9

Tulip Turquoise
CUT 12

Dark Green

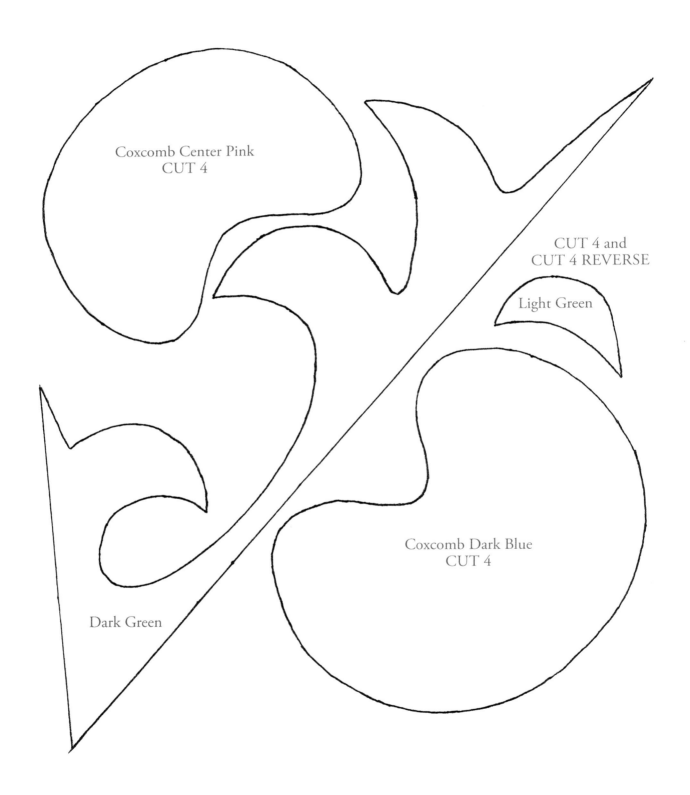

Coxcomb Center Pink
CUT 4

CUT 4 and
CUT 4 REVERSE

Light Green

Dark Green

Coxcomb Dark Blue
CUT 4

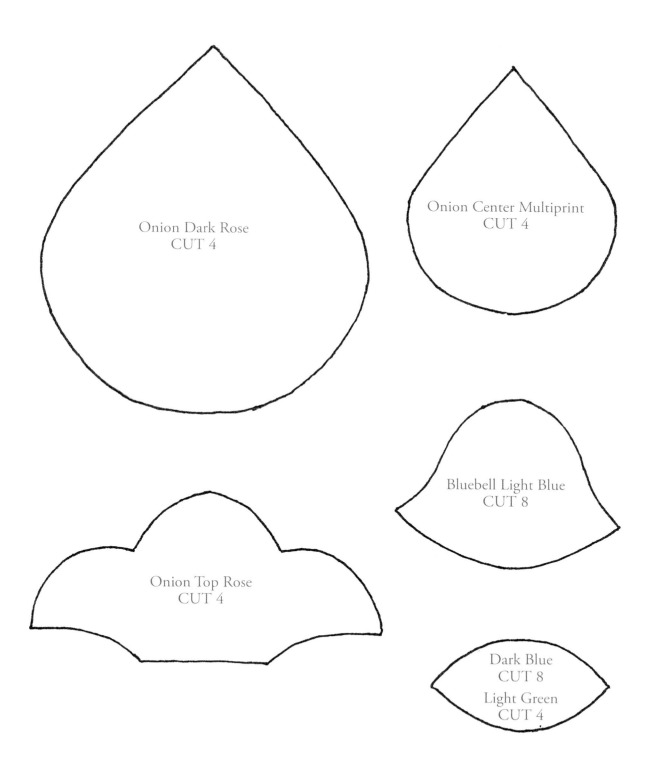

Onion Dark Rose
CUT 4

Onion Center Multiprint
CUT 4

Bluebell Light Blue
CUT 8

Onion Top Rose
CUT 4

Dark Blue
CUT 8
Light Green
CUT 4

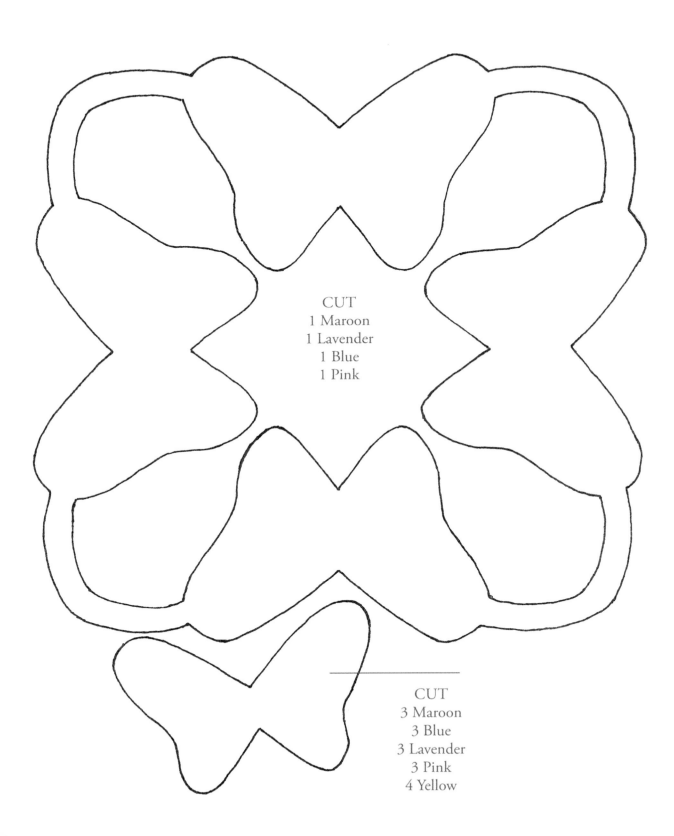

CUT
1 Maroon
1 Lavender
1 Blue
1 Pink

CUT
3 Maroon
3 Blue
3 Lavender
3 Pink
4 Yellow

# FOUR COLOR TULIPS

Center Leaf Pattern
CUT 4

Tulip
CUT 10 EACH
Light Blue
Dark Blue
Maroon
Pink

Green
CUT 4

# TAHITIAN DREAM

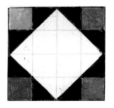

Block A

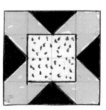

Block B

Tropical Print

CUT
5 Orange
5 Turquoise
4 Red
4 Lavender

# EXOTIC PURPLE LILY

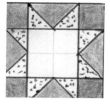

Block A

Block B

Tropical Print

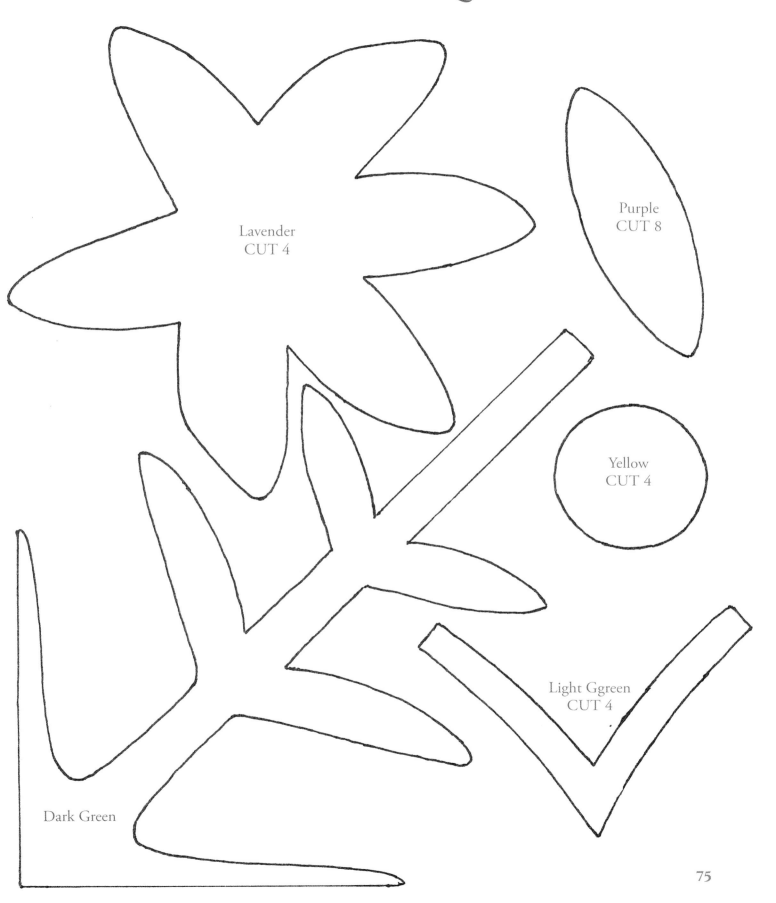

Lavender
CUT 4

Purple
CUT 8

Yellow
CUT 4

Light Ggreen
CUT 4

Dark Green

# AMAZING AMARYLLIS

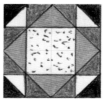

Block A          Block B          Tropical Print

# Amazing Amaryllis

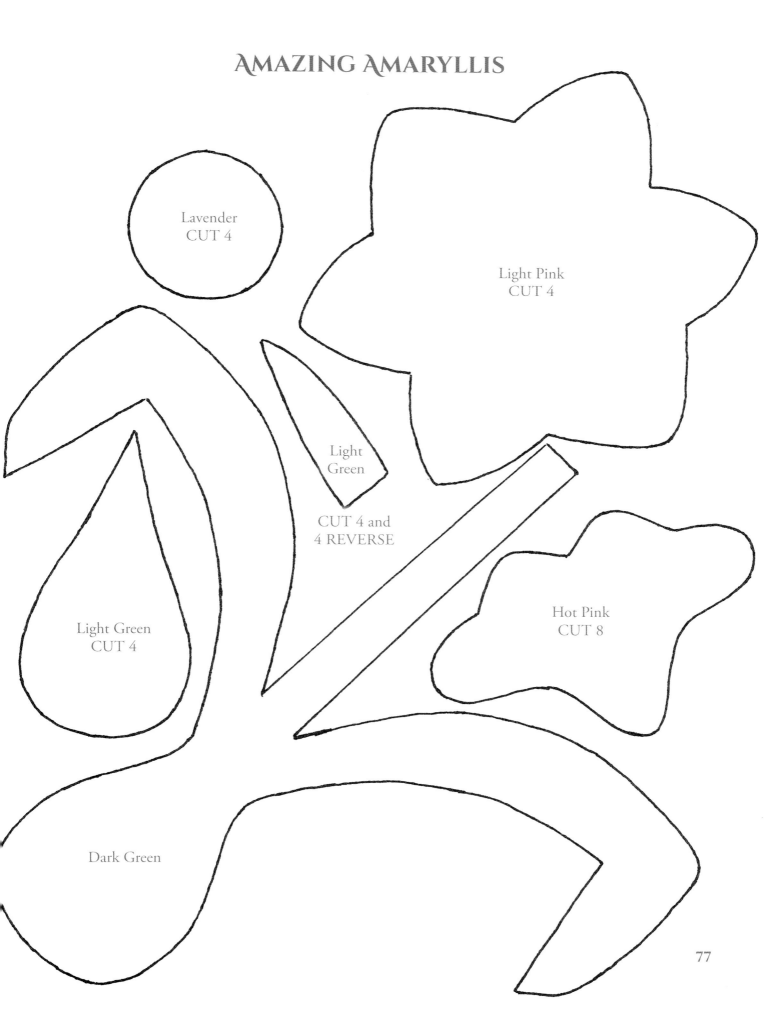

Lavender
CUT 4

Light Pink
CUT 4

Light Green

CUT 4 and
4 REVERSE

Light Green
CUT 4

Hot Pink
CUT 8

Dark Green

# DAFFODILS AND BLUEBIRDS

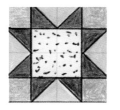

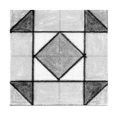

Block A                 Block B                 Tropical Print

Blue
CUT 4

Dark Green

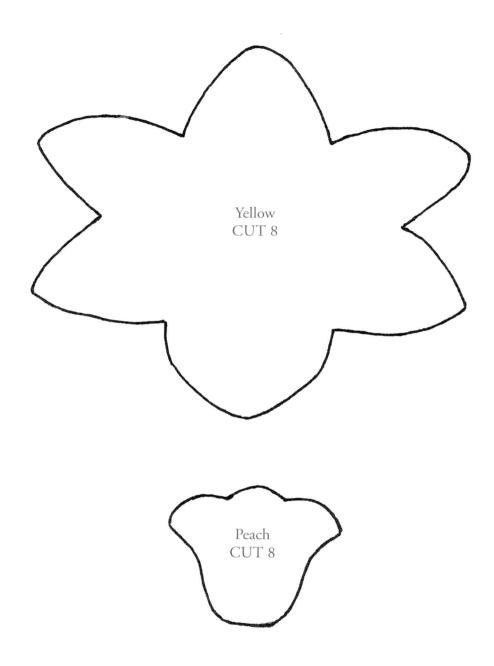

Yellow
CUT 8

Peach
CUT 8